Flourish

Kierra Wooden
Cover Design by Dontay Lockett

Kierra Wooden

Flourish

Acknowledgments

Writing Flourish was my journey intertwined with the lives of other women who are fighting to stand tall, fighting to show our beauty, fighting to be handled gently and with respect, fighting to be loved, and most importantly fighting to flourish.

I greatly appreciate the girls who shared their stories with me. You all opened up to me about things that held you back, that affected you drastically and how you overcame them. It inspired me during my journey of becoming whole.

To my friend Dakota thank you for encouraging me to make my dream of writing Flourish my reality. To my closest friends and family, I can't name you all but thank you for the unconditional support you all have given me. Thank you Dontay for designing my book cover and bringing my vision alive. To my mom thank you for always allowing me to be me and follow my dreams.

Contents

71. when you're in love
72. i'd go to war for u
73. first loves never fade
74. dandelion wishing
75. the child in me
76. super star
77. bloom
78. taken for granted
79. flourish

Flourish

Kierra Wooden

<u>shackled</u>

I let him inside my garden.
I showed him all the flowers I have grown:
Alyssums.
Amaryllis.
Freesias.
Iris.
Sunflowers.
Primroses.
Each of these sprouted through the success of tribulations.
I learned to water me in times of need.
With tears, I leaked I watered me, and out from the ground
grew me.
These flowers symbolize me.
I let him inside my garden.
He planted his seeds inside of me, and he told me he'd
water me.
He watered every flower that was a part of me,
and I grew, I grew so strong and my colors were vibrant.
I was yellow, I was red, I was white, I was green, I was
alive.
He was my sunshine, I bloomed facing him.
My colors were vibrant under his light.
I let him inside of my garden.
Because self-love wasn't enough, I wanted his love.
I wanted his love so bad, he planted roses around me
shackled me with thorns.
He said I had too much hope and he didn't.
He couldn't be my light anymore.
So, he snatched my:

Alyssums.
Amaryllis.
Freesias.
Iris.
Sunflowers.
Primroses.
Out the ground and even got the roots too.
I let him inside my garden and destroyed it.
Left me in the center shackled with thorns
and the remains of what use to be the petals of me.

<u>never enough</u>

"You're beautiful"
I hear it every day.
But I can't see it. I can't see it.
He gained interest in other girls and I can't even compare.
How am I possibly beautiful when he doesn't only see me?
I look in the mirror.
Staring at my reflection, pointing out the things he probably
didn't like about me.
Staring at myself till I became utterly disgusted in my
appearance.
I look at myself and break.
I wasn't enough, I never was enough
for him.

star girl

I'm going to become one with the stars in the sky.
One day.
I'm going to blow through lives like the wind.
I don't want to be remembered.
I'm going to be scattered across the earth like the dirt so the
world can keep walking all over me.
I'm going to wither away like the autumn leaves that falls
off trees
because nothing ever stays. — *real shit girl!*
I'm going to break like tree branches
because even the simplest things can collapse the strongest
foundations.
I'm going to be one with the stars in the sky tonight.

*my legacy will lye
in the constellations
above you all.*

<u>young heart</u>

Love has made me weak.
I've been biting my tongue
I've been torching my dreams.
I've forgotten about my wants and needs.
Because of this guy, I fell in love with.
He built me up and tore me down;
My confidence.
My heart.
My self-esteem.
Me…
And my young heart can't take it anymore.

i'm only hurting i

I'm only hurting because the person before broke my heart.
He's a bad habit I can't shake.
He's not good for my health.
I'm addicted to the pain it brings every time I see a picture
of him with her.
I'm addicted to the pain of realizing
Over
And
Over that I'm not his anymore.
And I fall apart.
Cause I know I'll never give him up.

i'm only hurting ii

I'm only hurting because the person before broke my heart.
He won't even speak to me like it's my fault.
He moved on like I never had his heart.
Like I wasn't the center of his universe.
I'm addicted to the pain it brings when you lose your best friend.
I'm addicted to the pain it brings knowing that it's really over.
And I fall apart
Cause I'm not her.

i'm only hurting iii

I'm only hurting because the person before broke my heart.
He's everywhere, because we left memories all over this
city.
As my eyes blink I see us at that park
sitting in the car parked in the parking lot
talking about our lives together.
I'm an addict to this pain,
I'm an addict to this pain.
I like the way it feels when my heartstrings break.
I like the way you give me pain.

<u>i'm only hurting iv</u>

I'm only hurting because the person before broke my heart.
And my limp grip is still holding on even though he moved on.
Holding on to that hope he'd say sorry to me one day.

<u>homesick</u>

Existing is becoming too much.
I'm tired of feeling low
even though I'm trying to keep my spirits high.
I'm tired of people with their selfish ways.
They take and take from me but will never give.
I'm tired of trying when nothing gets better.
I don't want to feel this anymore.
Existing is becoming too much.
I'm tired of closing my eyes and my vision is clouded with
things I regret.
Like I regret giving him that second chance
what if I did this instead
what if I said this
why didn't I say no?
I'm tired of people poking at my wounds that I warned
them of.
How fucked up of people to be aware of the pain you've
been through and have the nerve to hurt you.
I'm tired of the constant ache
treating everyone better than they treat me.
Existing has become too much.
I wanna go back home
I wanna go back home.
Back to the stars.
So, I can no matter what shine,
shine my brightest through all the darkness.
Because existing on this planet has become too much.
And I'm tired.

<u>soul tied</u>

My stem is all tangled with hers, with you.
My soul is tied to you, to her.
You gave her half of me.
You gave me half of her.
You got both of us.

- Soul tied

<u>unworthy</u>

I did everything you wanted.
Bowing down on my knees to please, even when you were
undeserving.
Showing gratitude to my king.
Meanwhile I was being deceived
telling lies to appease me,
so, you can appease her, and we.
I guess I wasn't enough, but you could have told me.
Instead you broke me down,
crushed my spirit,
made me cry till my eyes were wounds my tears were
blood pouring out.
And hell, I could've died,
at least that would put my pain at ease.
I go to sleep at night feeling like I am not deserving of a
love I gave you.
And I watch you create these false realities of we, of me...
I watch you continually lie on me to appease.
I did everything you wanted, but you always get what you
want and wanted.
And I shouldn't be to one with this grief of insecurity.
Wondering if I'm good enough for a love I gave you.

coyote woman i

You had an invader in our home that I made for us.
She left her scent all over it.
I stand outside, because I see you and her.
I see you look at her with love in your eyes.
I howled to moon
What I saw left me broken inside.
Our home is no longer my home
Our home is now you and hers.
Because she invaded it.

<u>coyote woman ii</u>

I watch in a bitter state
all those girls
you let mark their territory
in our home…

<u>thief</u>

You took the seed that made me whole.
It was what put light in my eyes,
life in my laugh,
hope in my smile.

I can't grow

autumn

Why can't you tell me the truth as to why you stopped
watering me?
I was shooting through the soil to get closer to you.
I was about to bloom for you, when the season was right.
I was growing just for you.
All you had to do was water me.
You snatched the roots of me out of your garden.
The hell with me huh?
I did it all for you, but you stopped watering me.
Didn't even give me a chance to see what I could be.
You wasted no time to leave,
summer is over and I'm dead with the leaves.

<u>wilt</u>

I'm losing myself quicker than the autumn leaves that falls off the branches of dying trees.

destroy me

Come on
just take what's left of me.
Pluck my petals,
peel my stem,
dig out my roots from the earth,
and rip me apart.
You never wanted me from the start.
Yet, you took the time to water me
bask me in the sun
And watch me grow.
Come on just take what's left.
I give up anyways.
I was hoping that my petals turn stale
my stem loses its balance
fall to its side.
You never wanted me anyways.

This is how it feels to be broken at 2AM

I clench my fist tight like an unbloomed cherry blossom.
Digging my nails deep into my flesh.
As memories of you, and her breaks my heart all over
again.
A pain that resurfaces when I'm wide awake at 2AM.
The anger I feel because I never knew
Never felt what it's like to be loved like the love I give.
Everyone takes from my home I made in me
because I leave the door open.
Love?
It was what made my home
but nobody ever gave it back in return.
Love?
It is gone.
Now I am empty wide awake at 2AM

<u>letter to mommy</u>

Dear Mommy,

I apologize for all you have to bear. I feel so hopeless,
wishing I can take some weight off your shoulders.
You deserve so much more. You didn't bring me in this
world alone.
You deserve so much more.
I feel so hopeless wishing I can take some weight off your
shoulders.
And I know I can be ungrateful and selfish at times.
But everything I do is for you.
One day I'll take the weight off your shoulders.
And give you everything your heart desire.
You deserve the world, not tired eyes!
You don't deserve to sacrifice every time!
You didn't bring me in the world alone.
But you didn't give up on me, you didn't push me to the
side like dad did.
Even at our worst you still gave us something a mother can
only give.
Unconditional love.
Everything I do is for you
one day I'll take the weight off your shoulders.

<u>daddy's guilt</u>

When you look at me do you see my mother?
Because daddy I have my mother's face when she was 18
and with you.
When you see me does it reminds you of how much you
hurt her?
Because you never seem to know how to love your
daughters,
just like you never seem to know how to love our mother.
Daddy I am 19 years old and you don't even know my
favorite color.
You don't know how great I'm doing in college.
You wear guilt on your face whenever you see your
daughters.
We come around, but you never seem to bother to sit and
talk to us, get to know us.
All 3 of us share our mother's face.
When you see us does it reminds you of how you broke our
mother?
You knew you didn't deserve her and your three beautiful
daughters.
But when we look at you daddy we see a coward.
We see everything we don't want for our daughters.
We see an example of a man we don't want our future
husbands to be.
Because when you look at us you see the face of our
mother when she was 18 and with you.

fatherless girls

I was always calling out to you.
Help guide one of the fatherless girls.
I was always trying to call,
I was always showing up for you,
but you were nowhere to be found.
I didn't know who to go to!
I didn't know who to go to!
Because I just wanted you, but you were nowhere to be found.
So, I use to go home and wait till everyone was asleep.
I used to sit on the bathroom floor, decorating my body in red, trying to get closer to you.
Leaving voicemails in these wounds,
Sacrificing my blood, but still you wouldn't show up.
So, I used a whole bottle of pills, so I could talk to you.
But mommy caught me trying to get closer to you.
I put up a fight, hurting myself hoping it hurt you.
I wanted you to talk to me, tell me it was okay.
So, I kept my knees black and blue looking up at the moon.
They said that's where you live, up there.
You left me here without a warning,
without a guide.
You're just like my fucking father.
He ran away from his problems.
And they say I'm running away from mine.
But it's not true I just wanted to talk to you God.
I just wanted to see if I look just like you.
Because they say we are created in your image.

I can't help but see the man who planted a seed in my
mother
and guilt refrain him from looking at what he grew.

<u>Monica's poem i</u>

Why did you have to leave me?
You took my sanity away from me.
I need my mother
to lead me
to heal me
to love me
complete me.
I was the lily that grew from your womb.
You were my root.
And life snatched you away.
My sanity?
Mommy it was you.

Punnett squares

It kept coming late, but we didn't mind.
Making Punnett Squares in my mind.
It was going to be all mine,
With my eyes, and your nose, my hair, and your lips.
Till that moment hit
this can possibly be true.
We didn't care if it happened, we loved each other enough
that we didn't care if the seeds inside of me were possibly
growing.
Till that moment hit
this can possibly be true.
It was late, and I needed you.
Sitting in that waiting room, waiting for you.
Making Punnett Squares in my mind.
It was going to be all mine,
With my eyes, and your nose, my hair, and your lips.
But you never came,
and this can possibly be true.
They called my name.
Still. No. You.
I needed you.
I left the office, overflowing with thorns.
Still I haven't heard from you.
I was terrified, was it time? And I picked the wrong guy.
I wanted to die and take you with me.
It would just be me and you.
With my hair and my eyes.
My womb was filled with rose petals that left me poisoned.
My womb was full and twisted.

You couldn't grow.
You spilled out of me.

<u>rape</u>

Between my legs is not a field you can run through,
snatching flowers off their stems, clenching tight petals of
what remains.

<u>world war i</u>

Careful not to whimper as you're sitting against the
bathroom door.
Don't make a sound as you take some pain away.
It's okay.
Do it till you exhale in relief.
Watch the pain escape out the slits in raspberry showers.
Wipe your tears with your aching hands.
Stand up and feel the stings on your fragile legs.
You look in the mirror and your eyes remind you of your
self-inflicted wounds.
You tiptoe back to your bedroom.
In the morning, you're going to decorate your arms in
wristbands.
The world can't know you're fighting a battle.
A battle against them.
So, you hide your battle scars.
You question if being alive is even worth it cause you're
gonna die one day, eventually.
So, you're just waiting for the day you actually cut deep
enough and slowly slip away.
Exhale in relief and slowly slip away.

girls at war

They laugh at us
They laugh at us
They see how far we go
They see us viciously attack each other
They see us plotting on the kill
They laugh at us
They see how far we go
When us girls tear each other apart
For their hearts they don't even want
To give us.

tear stained asphalt

I dropped to the ground with a silent thud.
I lied there to face the sky.
Tears splashing the asphalt and I feel like I just died.
The silent breeze, and those raspy leaves mocked my
sorrow.
My heart beat tempo was dying as my heart broke through
the seams.
I was never alive, so I can't be revived.
I was living death
and my teardrops were mess.
My heartbeat was a painful song no one listen too.
Cause a silent thud hit the asphalt.
Nobody cared, they buried her in shame.
And her tears are stains that will forever remain.
Because it stayed
It never will fade.
But no one ever felt its pain.

<u>hate</u>

I hate this poem because it's about you, you, you and you!

suicides hotline

Suicide knocks at my door.
It mimics the
anger
hurt
distrust
I have against the world.
Suicide tells me it's easy
"just swallow many pills"
"slit open your wrist"
Then everything that has hurt you will be gone.
Suicide? I don't have the guts to do it.
I try sometimes.
Then I realize I'm not ready to die!
Cause if I commit suicide where will I go?
What will be left of me?
Will I die a sin?
Suicide!
It's always on my mind!
Always knocking on my doors persuading me to take the
easy way out.

set her free

He shot an angel.
He shot his angel that was there to save him.
She loved him.
Her white gown was stained with the blood that rushed
through her veins for him.
He said hush little angel the pain will fade.
He said hush little angel close your eyes I swear this
fucking pain will fade.
He didn't want her anymore.
He let demons disguised as saints fool him.
He shot an angel.
He shot his angel that was there to save him.
She loved him.
He didn't want to stay.
He didn't want to clean up the mess he made.
He let demons in-
They took his soul.
His angel bled out all her glory, her love, her innocence.
Now she's one of the soulless ghouls that ghost the streets.
Because he shot an angel that was there to save him.
He should've set her free.
He should've set her free.

I didn't give you permission

I'm always that girl.
The ones men try to take advantage of.
The one who's too friendly and men take it the wrong way.
My smile doesn't mean you can touch me.
My laugh doesn't mean you can touch me.
My small talk doesn't mean you can touch me.
You can't touch me, you can't touch me.
You can't touch me there.
    - I didn't give you permission to touch me there.
I'm always that girl.
The ones men try to take advantage of.
They always say scream, they always say "Just Say No",
they always say fight back.
How?
When my voice muted.
When my tears couldn't fall.
When my body froze.
Because he knew what he was doing was wrong.
Yet he still gropes me there, he grinded up against me
there.
Who told you, who told you, you could touch me there?
You can't touch me there!
You can't touch me there!
    - I didn't give you permission to touch me there.

<u>little woman</u>

They told me I was a woman at 10 years old when blood stained my Barbie panties.

stoned

Did you know they use to stone women like us for being dirty?
But the dirty men who steals virginities were throwing the stones.
My blood on his hands.
My blood on the crotch of my dress.
I'm a dirty woman.
Cause he took the only thing I have control over.
So, all the men in town see me unwed with blood running down my legs.
Throwing stones.
Screaming out "Whore"
But can't they see that I did not want it?
Did you know they use to kill women like us for being dirty?

<u>unrequited</u>

I couldn't get into it.
Forcefully tugging at my buds.
My body knows what love feels like, and you couldn't give
me that.
My body laid lifeless under you, waiting for you to reach
your climax.
I feel empty inside.

<u>coward</u>

I apologize to the girls who were publicly harassed by the dangerous men who lurk the streets.
I apologize for the fear I get for speaking up for you, though it is my place to defend you.
Because men will speculate your altercation with those dangerous men, but never defend you. Never say "ay man leave her alone!" Out of the respect that you are someone's daughter, you could be their daughter.
I apologize to you because I am you, I've been in the same position as you.
And it burns fire in me to see people stare at you and laugh because the guy is fucking crazy, but they mute you crying for help!
I apologize, I let fear consume me, I am a coward.
Because you, you are me.
It is my place to defend you and I let you down, just like you let me down, but worst of all they let us down.
The men, who watch us cry for help.

unworthy ii

Coming to the realization they don't really want me.
They just want to fuck me.
Because I'm talking and it's like they're not listening
because they'll try to distract me with meaningless kisses,
that leads to them trying to stick their hands down my
pants.
Pretending like they get me, so they can have my lotus...
Though this hurts me because I don't feel worthy of what
I'm capable of giving.

<u>chlorophyll</u>

Do you think since I'm pretty that means my life is easy?
I should be happy I have all these admirers.
Men throwing flower petals at my feet.
Begging to be with me. Since I'm pretty.
But they never take the time to admire what's within.
Never shine the light right for my chlorophyll.
I am more than physical beauty.
I am phenomenal within.
Too phenomenal to waste time chasing guys who only want
what's on the outside and only care about my insides if
they can stick their manhood inside.
Do you think since I'm pretty that means my life is easy?
Because I can't seem to phantom if I'll ever find the one
who wants me, to shine their light right for my chlorophyll.

judgement day

They judge me for not believing in you.
They judge me for questioning you.
Because I can't seem to understand you.
You give my existence less meaning because you take all
the credit for everything I do.
You say our purpose is to serve you. So I'm a slave to you.
Because everything I do is to meet you.
They judge me for not believing in you.
So, I'm damned.
I guess I'll never meet you.

<u>cramps</u>

I feel my uterus mocking motherhood.

-Cramps

<u>can i be her? i</u>

Can I be her?
I want to bloom in full perfection for you.
But some of my petals hang loose,
Is that okay with you?
Can I be her?
I want to bloom in full perfection for you.
But my colors are a little dull,
Is that okay with you?
Can I be her?
I want to bloom in full perfection for you.
I know I'm not the roses you love to pick.
But can you grow to love the iris?
She blooms to be loved by you.

can i be her? ii

I make wishes on dandelions about you.
Wishing you see me like I see you.
Hoping the seed, I blew lands on you.
I accept all that you are,
I made wishes hoping you accept me for everything I am.
Because I blow wishes hoping I can be the one
To help mend any wounds in you.
Wishing I can be the one
For you.
Can I be her?

i'm not her.

Did my feelings bloom too early for you?
Is this season an inconvenience for you?
I'm sorry I didn't mean too.
It's okay if you don't feel the same way as I do.
My petals will wither away soon.
Because I've bloomed feelings for boys
Who didn't want much from me anyway.
And my petals will wither away.
Because I'm not her.

drown me

You don't have to lie, you don't have to pretend.
I know what it feels like to be the only one to fall in.
It's okay you don't have to pretend.
I've been kissed by boys who didn't want much
From me.
They all drowned me.

beautiful trash

I am walking on sidewalks where hearts were broken,
I'm looking into eyes that are ghosted.
I was kissed by murders…
I am a victim of bad romance.
I'm looking at my reflection in train windows, dirty glass
of abandoned storefronts.
It's my true reflection, all that beauty under so much ugly.

<u>white tail Moscato</u>

Today nobody tried to force me to consume it.
Nobody was looking when I poured the remains in the
glass.
As I sipped slowly feeling the slight burns in my chest.
I think I like it, made me feel like a woman, more in
control, more bold.
White Tail Moscato running through my blood streams.
It might become my favorite drink.
I don't want to feel what I'm feeling.
White Tail Moscato shielding me with fiery energy around
my heart.
I want to escape within its sweet and bitter taste.
Because these tears won't fall under her spell she's casted
in me.
She won't let me feel pain.
Today nobody tried to force me to consume it.
Nobody was looking when I sipped slowly feeling the
slight burns in my chest.
The beginning of beautiful messy mess.

sexual abandon

You were the only one
to make my center explode.
Make my body feel
like it was under your control.
Sweat dripping down your face
landing on parts of me.
Roses blossomed
On all my soft spots.
You were the only one
to make me sing.
Made me feel safe
To be me,
So, I stopped caring about how loud I screamed.
You were the only one.
You were supposed to be
The only one.
You abandoned me
Left me an empty shell.
Cause I haven't felt safe
In arms of others.
It was just you.
Cause you were the one

<u>promiscuous girl</u>

Your legs spread when he caresses your insecurities.
You undress your serenity.
You do all the things he wants, forcing waterfalls.
You'd do anything to not feel lonely.
Letting him enter, as he places a kiss on your lips, is this
what it feels like to be complete?
-
When you blink your eyes
Guy, after guy. How many? it's been over five.
You look in the mirror over the bathroom sink. Splashing
cold water on your face.
"Why don't you love me? Why don't you love me? Why
don't you love me? Why don't you love me? Why don't
you love me? Why don't you love me?" Is all you repeat
numbly.
Losing yourself in each guy you let undress your serenity.
You search for love in promiscuity but never from yourself.
How are they gonna love you when you can't love
yourself?
Guy, after guy.
You'll never find yourself by breaking your own heart.
You won't find the love you'd want for yourself through
orgasms and sweet talk.
Promiscuous girl, they'll never love you.

honey on my bones

He poured honey on my bones to sweeten the pain.
Temporary bliss through each thrust, each kiss, honey
drips.
Piecing my bones back together in the dark of my bedroom,
never seen the light of sun during the process.
Kissing up my spine, honey sticking me together.
Kissing up my navel, between my breast, up to my neck
and my lips.
I am now whole again.
Honey sticks.
But
Honey doesn't hold forever.
Because when the sun rose honey leaked, my bones drifted
away in agony, you weren't there, gone into the thin air.
Temporary bliss through each thrust, each kiss, honey
drips.

<u>i think ily</u>

Do you remember what happened before we turned the
lights off?
You admired every part of me, told me I was beautiful.
My checks were on fire. I felt warm in my heart and
between my legs.
When you turned the lights off
You found my body in the dark.
You entered me with ease,
you caressed me,
you kissed me,
had me promise all of me was all yours.
Taking your time to please me, teaching me things I never
knew I could do.
Each time you got me to my climax I felt like I was
bursting with confetti.
We kept going till the birds were chirping.
I was bursting.
I didn't want it to end.
My heart was throbbing with forbidden feelings.

say you love me

Say you love, love, love me.
Ignite my fire,
bring me back to life
love me, love me.
please...
I say I love you and I cringe,
I forgot you wouldn't say it back.

is it really there?

I question
is it really there?
Screaming your name into thin air.
You bring me to my knees
baby
You bring me to my knees.
Scarlet knees,
Poseidon strikes my tear ducts
tears come in streams.
Is it really there?
Love comes with ease
love comes in abundance
love is timeless.
I question why I pour
and you're always empty.
Is it really there?
Is it really there?
I love u more than u love me

graveyard

Searching for wrong
because I know the end must come.
digging our grave
ready
for goodbye.
I cry, because I want u I need u.
I dig the grave because I'm used to
the end.
The end always comes.

<u>heart on my sleeve</u>

I wore my heart on my sleeve for you, I decorated it in red roses.
You said it was your favorite accessory of mine.
So, whenever I saw you, I'd show it off to you.
I wore it specially for you
So, whenever we talked, I'd send you selfies to show it off to you.
Don't you like how I wear my heart on my sleeve for you?
I ripped it out my chest,
For you,
Just to not realize that I'm wearing it for you.

lost faith

I used to talk to her
When heartbreaks felt like the world caving in.
When broken promises turned to tally marks on my wrist.
When my daddy rejected my phone calls confused me.
When I never realized all the scars inflicted on my mother.
I never understood how she could stomach watching what
she created going through hurricanes from the penthouse
cloud.
I stopped talking to her
When love made me forget about myself.
When I couldn't fill enough tally marks on my wrist.
When my daddy comes around and don't know how to talk
to us.
When my mother scars revealed themselves to me.
She watches from her penthouse cloud at all the hurricanes
she creates.
She watches from her penthouse cloud with a smile on her
face.
I can't believe in a God who feeds off pain.

i remember my first love

I remember my first love, love, love-
I remember my first love.
I clung onto it for dear life. Because I needed, needed love.
I clung onto him for dear life. Because I needed, needed him.
I didn't feel alive unless I was by his side. Because I was dead inside.
I recreated myself to fit his vision.
I recreated myself to fit his vision.
I remember my first love, love, love-
I hated the girl he wanted me to be.
I was not her.
I clung onto it for dear life. Because I needed, needed love.
I clung onto him for dear life. Because I needed, needed him.
I hated the girl he wanted me to be:
Submissive, obedient, quiet, silenced.
I remember my first love.
I loved the way he prided me like I was his trophy.
I loved the way he looked at me like he'd pour out.
I loved the way he always wanted me to be by his side every single moment
I hated how he never seemed to listen when I poured my heart out.
I hated how self-centered he was.
I hated how he take his anger out on me, and I took it. Then he made love to me and said sorry.
I loved the way he took care of me.
I loved the way he broke when we weren't okay.
I loved the way he needed me.
I remember my first love, love, love-
But I hated the girl I was.

Because I was not her.
I am more, I am love, I am understanding, I am intelligent,
I am talented, I am beautiful.
And that is who I am.
I remember my first love.
I clung onto it for dear life. Because I needed, needed love.
I clung onto him for dear life. Because I needed, needed
him.
For the fear of being lonely,
I remember my first love, love, love.
But the girl he wanted me to be.
I was not her.

it's just not my time

I understand it's not my time.
So, I should stop feeling bitter
vile up in my throat at the sight
of lovers holding hands.
So, I should stop letting loneliness
Sit on my shoulders and spit
Rose thorns in my ears because
the sounds are deafening when
I can't hear the words I love you
from another.
So, I should stop breaking my
own heart trying to find love
from each guy I give a chance.
I understand it's just not my time.

self-love is real love

I'm searching for real love.
Because I deserve that.
I'm desperate for it,
I try to find it in guys,
guys that I didn't really like.
Searching for something
I never really had.
I never felt it.
But it was something I took
Out of my chest and wrapped
It up and tied it in a bow
Hoping I got one in return.
I never did.
Still I search for real love.
Or maybe I should just
Start loving myself.
Fuck

__infertility i__

One day a flower will grow out the desert sand.
Its seed will blow through the dry breeze and have strength
to grow through infertility.

Poseidon's daughter

You hurt me, and Poseidon will strike down his trident.
Tsunami and hurricanes will scream your name and wash
you into the sea.
And there you will sink.
You hurt me, and Poseidon will strike down his trident.
And I'll ride the waves of your riptide where you scream.

storm chaser

You can't save me.
You can't stop me.
But you can chase me.
Or get swept in my winds, drown in my rain.
But you will never catch me.
I got places to be.
I'm a storm, I'm worse than rain.
You can't save me.
I'd murder anyone who get in my way.
I'm a storm, I'm worse than rain.
Stop trying to save me.
Stop trying to stop me.
It's dangerous to love me.

<u>infertility ii</u>

I vividly remember what it felt like when I knew I was
losing you.
I was drowning in the blood that seeped through the cracks
of my broken heart.
You weeded me out to make room for your new pretty
flower.
But kept pieces of me in case you wanted to have me again.
You knew all the right things to say to get me to rise from
the ground you stomped me in.
Because you knew no matter what I was the only one
native to your land.
Whenever you got bored of your new pretty flower that you
leave sitting in a glass vase filled with water.
You always try to come back to the real you.
-
My seeds can no longer grow for you.
You continuously ripped me from the roots.
Now my seeds don't recognize this infertile land.
I am no longer your native you selfish man.

<u>sunflower</u>

They never stick around long enough,
to see me fully bloom.
They got tired of waiting,
waiting for my stem to shot out but wouldn't water me.
They got tired of waiting,
waiting for my petals to burst through the bud but wouldn't
bathe me in the sun.
They got tired of waiting, waiting to see how vibrant
I've become, but wouldn't try to understand
I'm more than what meets the eye, I'm a process with depth.
If you would have stuck around long enough you would
have known I'm yellow like the sun, and I'm strong because
my stem is 6 feet tall facing the sun, my petals are soft like
pillow kisses, I'm intelligent, my seeds spread vitality.
If you would have stuck around you would have known
I was broken, for a long time.
Until I found hope in the sun,
and now that's why when I bloom,
I bloom facing the sun.

she was God

I knew God couldn't exist when
she took her own life.
She did only what a God could do.
She didn't want to be here anymore,
And I respect that.
She was my angel, my soulmate.
And I wonder lifelessly without her
Because I'm incomplete.
But it's what she wanted,
And I respect that.
She gave me some of the best years of my life.
And hell, I wished she would have took me with her!
I've been standing in the rain.
I wonder if this is how she cries.
Because I know she didn't mean to hurt me but she
couldn't take it no more here.
And it hurts because I wonder
If she realized she was my world.
She was my soulmate.
I hope one day I see her again,
I hope she save me a spot in the sky.
Because I see her star twinkling every night.
At least I know you're at peace.
A true friend you, have my heart to keep.

Monica's poem ii

I found you mommy.
I see the weather.
You're the sun that dried my tears.
The rain that wash away my fears.
The storm when I rumble.
The cold that keeps me contained.
I found you mommy.
In the clouds that hover over me.
You keep the ground level steady under my feet.
'Cause when I fall, I look up and follow.
I found you mommy.
You're Mother Earth I see the weather.

<u>learning to stand tall</u>

I was breaking limbs
making myself small
to stand tall on your level
"I'd do anything for u
but can I be yours?"
Not yet
it's not time
soon
yet I wondered why?
I was breaking more
limbs and you were towering
over I.
I was worthy before I began
breaking myself apart.
"I deserve better than this
I can't do this anymore"

<u>i'm all i need</u>

How do you find the strength to continue to grow when all
they ever did was pluck at your petals, peel at your stem,
and break you down the middle?
How do you find it in you to still love the same?
I watched your soil dry and crumble quenched with thirst
for love.
And you replied:
I have enough water inside of me to water me, I love me
enough and I'm all I need.

<u>when you're in love</u>

Grab hold of my hand.
I can take you away
to a better place
where love pours like rain.
And in my arms is a waterfall.
We surrender to butterflies
when we're feeling unsure.
And red roses grow whenever we
look at each other.
The sun makes us realize that
we're alive.
And I burst in ultraviolet rays
radiating you with something real.
The moon shines bright at night
when it hears how beautiful you
can make me sing.
The birds chirp on the windowsill
the morning after cause they
adore the beauty of our love.
Grab hold of my hand.
I can take you away
to a better place.

i'd go to war for u

I dreamt of bodies
colliding
panting
looking into each other eyes.
Exploring ways to
define love.
Feelings inspired by
dirty talk, bite marks,
passion, kissing,
purple bruises.
It was war, it was war.
I dreamt of bodies
colliding
at war with each other
for love...
"Tell me I'm yours, I wanna be yours"
biting of tongues
stop biting tongues
conform to your heart
I'm yours, u want me to be yours.
I dreamt of war
to be loved by u
bodies colliding
I'd go to war for u.

first loves never fade

I wonder what it will be like
when we see each other again.
Will our memories flood your brain?
bring you to your knees?
Will our memories flood my brain?
make me weak?
Because I can hear the echo
"I can't live without you"
You said it too. It was what you wanted.
I meant it I was ready to find paradise
in the sky.
My life was gonna end with you.
I wonder what it will be like
when we see each other again.
Will you be wrapped up in the one
that has your heart?
Will you walk past trying hard not
to look my way?
because we both know
I always had your attention.
Cause first loves cut deepest
but they never fade.
They remain because we were
each other's first real true love.
But it was what you wanted.
To go our separate ways.
And maybe our hearts will
find paradise in the sky one day.
From the pain first love gives.

dandelion wishing

Remember how we thought getting older would mean something?
And that we'd have each other till death do us part?
When we were 14 having fantasies about what it be like to turn 17.
We'd both have a broken heart, we'd cry to each other in a toxic state, mascara running down her flushed face, singing Lana Del Rey.
Till death do us part, till death do us part.
Remember when you got your license at 16 and we planned to take your moms car and travel the country for the summer?
We'd have the windows rolled down, screaming lyrics to our favorite throwbacks, laughing for no reason, maybe it's because freedom makes you feel some type of way. It felt good, it felt like a dream to escape in fantasies with you.
Till death do us part, till death do us part.
We're both 20 now you go to college out of state and I stayed.
I haven't seen you in months, but we wished each other a happy birthday. That was all.
I kinda wish that we could be teenagers a little while longer. Because I'd still have you a little bit longer.
Instead we made dandelion wishes to be older, and we floated away from each other.
We landed in different paths and grew apart.

Kierra Wooden

the child in me

I had to keep you trapped inside of my rib cage to protect
you from the harshness of the world.
You kept kicking,
screaming, begging
I set you free.
I'm sorry but 20-year-old me
can't chase after honey bee's
life isn't sweet.
I'm sorry but 20-year-old me
can't cry when the world is mean to me
everyone isn't friendly.
The child in me, I can't set you free.
But I offer you freedom in my dreams.
Though, there are days when I can't sleep.
I beg to her to let me sleep
to close my eyes from this nightmare.
You kick, you scream
you kick, you scream
my ribs have cracks, but I'll heal.
The child in me I can't set you free
you're the only part of me worth keeping.

super star

If I could look death in her eyes
I think I might smile.
Because life did me wrong.
I lost my will to go on.
I've been laying in a bed of thorns.
Sinking in,
smiling as each prick digs in.
I tried, I tried, I tried.
Will be my last words.
Cause I use to cry to her in
the middle of the night.
I'm trying, I'm trying, I'm trying.
Life just kept doing me wrong.
Put me back with the stars
So, I can be the shooting stars
in the lives of the broken
that made wishes for everyone to be
happy but themselves.
That beg in the middle of the
night for happiness.
I'll be that shooting star.
If I could look death in her eye
I think I might smile.

Kierra Wooden

<u>bloom</u>

You gave me the best seasons of my life.
At least I got to experience all the holidays with you,
New Year's too.
You helped me unravel to reveal what was underneath.
Too bad you couldn't meet her.
You probably would have loved her even more.
But you gave me the strength to stand tall on my own.
To water myself with self-love.
Revealing what's underneath.
You gave me the best seasons of my life.
Though you destroyed me in the summer, left me scorned,
my petals drying in your heatwave.
My seeds found strength to bloom again.

<u>taken for granted</u>

When you take me for granted
have fun
selfishly hogging all the sun
I hope you were warm
while I waited in the storm.
when you took me for granted
you ran through the sun rays
and drug me through the mud
you looked over when you tugged
and I didn't budge.
I released your hand and walked away
the sun will shine for me
but not with you.

flourish

It's spring again-
My Alyssums, Amaryllis, Freesias, Iris, Sunflowers and
Primroses stand strong again.
And I stand in the center crowned assembled in Gorse
flowers.
My garden is open to the world, like Mother Earth.
And everyone I meet plant a seed in me. and I grow flowers
I never knew I could be.
I spread my love to everyone I meet I'm so full of it.
And they all water me.
I'm red, I'm green, I'm purple, I'm pink, I'm yellow, I'm
free. Free from the shackles because I am loved, loved so
dearly by me and the world.
Alyssums, Amaryllis, Freesias, Iris, Sunflowers and
Primroses stand strong again.
Because I am Mother Earth, I still grow, I still nourish, I'm
still colorful, still beautiful no matter how much negativity
people try to plant in me.
I flourish.

Made in the USA
Lexington, KY
28 April 2018